Old ELIE and EARLSFERRY

by
Eric Eunson

Andrew Greig established a cycle business in Elie in 1886, branching into motor car repairs in the early years of this century. The garage buildings in Chapman's Wynd shown in this 1920s photograph were built in 1905. By the 1920s the firm were advertising closed and open motors for hire by the hour, day, week or month, and had private lock-ups for rent in Ferry Road and Chapman's Place.

© Stenlake Publishing 1999
First published in the United Kingdom, 1999,
by Stenlake Publishing Ltd.
Telephone: 01290 551122
www.stenlake.co.uk

ISBN 1 84033 072 4

The publishers regret that they cannot supply
copies of any pictures featured in this book.

SELECT BIBLIOGRAPHY

Brodie, Ian, *Steamers of the Forth*, 1976
Corstorphine, James, *East of Thornton Junction*
Fife Golfing Association, *A History of Golf Clubs in Fife*
Gifford, John, *The Buildings of Scotland, Fife*, 1988
Hay Fleming, D., *Guide to the East of Fife*, 1886
Pride, Glen, *The Kingdom of Fife, An Illustrated Architectural Guide*, 1990
Russell, C. S., *The East Fife Observer, 1914-1939*
Silver, Owen, *The Roads of Fife*, 1987
Wood, Walter, *The East Neuk of Fife*, 1887

Statistical Accounts, Parishes of Elie (1794-1795 & 1836)
and Kilconquhar (1792 & 1837) and Elie & Earlsferry, 1951.

INTRODUCTION

Both Elie and Earlsferry, and the estates associated with them, originally belonged to the parish of Kilconquhar. The largest parish in the East Neuk, it once reached from the Cocklemill Burn on the west to Coal Farm near St Monans on the east, and inland to Largoward.

Earlsferry appears to be the older settlement, and tradition ascribes the origin of its name to Macduff, Earl of Fife, being ferried across the Forth here by local fishermen as he fled the wrath of Macbeth (King of Scotland from 1040 to 1057). It is also said that after this event he persuaded Malcolm III (1058-1093) to impose a ruling that the pursuers of any fugitive crossing at Earlsferry must wait on the shore until their quarry was half-way across the firth before continuing their chase. However, the perpetuation of this and other tales relating to Macduff in Fife probably derive from aspects of Shakespeare's writings becoming interwoven with Scottish history; there is no firm evidence to confirm that Macduff actually existed, and the succession of the Earls of Fife is well documented.

In 1177 Duncan, Earl of Fife, confirmed a grant made by his father, also Duncan (d., 1154), of a hospital and associated lands to the Convent of North Berwick. The remains of this building, or a successor to it, can still be seen at the west end of Earlsferry. This hospital was not a place of healing, but a resting place for wayfarers and pilgrims, and a similar foundation was established on the opposite shore at North Berwick. It is not improbable that it was one of these Duncans (both Earls of Fife), who established a ferry between these hospitals from which the town derives its name.

William I (1165-1214) granted the lands of Ardross (which included much of what was later to become the estate and town of Elie) to one Merleswain, a nobleman of Saxon descent whose family also possessed extensive properties at Kennoway. Waldef, son of Merleswain of Ardross, was in possession of the estate of Kincraig in the same period, and he granted a charter to the Convent of North Berwick of the common pasture or links of Kincraig with the provision 'that Connac shall be removed from his cell, that is, the hospital, so that none of my men shall hereafter dwell nearer to the said land, than the men of the convent'. A 'salina' or salt pan is also mentioned on these lands, one of the earliest references to what would later become a staple industry on the Forth. The manufacture of salt by evaporating sea water required coal, and from this fact it can be deduced that coal was also being worked in the vicinity at this early date. Earlsferry is not recorded in a grant confirming the nuns' properties by Malcolm, Earl of Fife, dated 1228, which refers only to 'the hospital lands of Ardross', but a document of 1295 refers to the muir of 'the hospital of Earlsferry'. It is thought the burgh was founded and acquired its name between these dates. Between 1366 and 1368 most of the extensive Ardross estate came into the possession of Sir William Dishington, and his son of the same name built Ardross Castle before 1400.

The town of Elie is of indeterminate age and the origin of its name is obscure. The first mention of the harbour is dated 1586 and comes from the memoirs of James Melville, who describes landing at 'the Ailie' after a nightmarish crossing of the Forth. In 1587 Thomas Dishington of Ardross erected Elie into a free burgh, port and haven. Earlsferry, it seems, was the more important place and was elevated to the status of a royal burgh in 1589, when it was described as 'old beyond the memory of man'. However, shortly before in 1572 it was reported that the town was 'reduced to nothing' and the ferry was almost defunct, possibly as a consequence of the cessation of pilgrimages to St Andrews after the recent Reformation. Ardross was abandoned as a residence some time during the sixteenth century and by 1598 the Dishingtons had moved their seat inland to Carmurie. This mansion stood a short way east of Broomlees Farm, but even less now remains of it than the 'rickle of stanes' that was Ardross.

In 1598 Sir Thomas Dishington sold Wester Ardross, also styled 'the Elie', to William Scott, later knighted, who had previously bought Muircambus and East Newton Rires in 1594. The area sold comprised 'Carmurie, especially Labernal, Drumis and Lochquharney' and 'the Over Links of Ardross, the town of Elie, the Law, Swarf and Mill of Elie and the Nether Links of Ardross'. In 1611 Scott acquired the remaining portion of Ardross, and bequeathed the sum of five thousand merks towards the cost of building a church in Elie in 1630. His son, also Sir William, provided the site for the building, and upon its completion in 1639 annexed all his lands to it and had them erected into the new parish of Elie. Owing to his desire to have all his properties in the parish, Elie had the odd distinction of having three detached portions, namely Muircambus, East Newton Rires and Bruntsheils, the last of these eight miles from the rest of the parish! The forerunner of the present Elie House was built around the beginning of the seventeenth century by one of the two Sir William Scotts (it is not clear which). The family was much impoverished by the Civil War and in 1697 the bulk of the Elie estates were acquired by Sir William Anstruther.

The last substantial estate in the area was Sandford, known since the nineteenth century as St Ford. From the fifteenth century Sandford was in the hands of the Duddingston family. The estate included Broomlees and three other farms no longer extant which were known as Wellbank, Langfauld and Greysland, but these were sold in 1690. They were acquired by the Anstruthers of Elie in 1720 and Sandford itself followed suit in 1765.

Elie began to increase in importance during the seventeenth century and several fine townhouses were built during this period, notably the residence of David Nairne on the east side of Rankeillor Street, which dates from 1604, and others in South Street of which only carved stones and doorways incorporated in later buildings survive. In 1670 Elie was granted the right to hold three annual fairs, and its established weekly market was changed from the Sabbath to Tuesday. In 1755 the population of Elie was 642, but this had fallen to 620 by 1790, probably as a consequence of agricultural improvements carried out by Sir John Anstruther. A number of small farms, notably those earlier associated with Carmurie and Broomlees, were amalgamated at this time.

In 1794 Elie had seven square-rigged vessels of 1,000 to 1,100 tons burden, all employed in foreign trade, and one sloop used as a coaster. Ships were also being built in the town at the time. William Steel is named as a shipbuilder at Elie in 1821, but the business was extinct by 1836. The harbour, though, was described in 1794 as going fast to ruin. In the same year, the Rev. William Pairman mentions the growing popularity of Elie as a sea-bathing resort. One of the first places in Fife to be noted as such, this is the first hint of Elie's appeal to tourists which was to become its primary role within a century.

The Leith and Aberdeen Steam Yacht Co.'s vessels *Tourist* and *Velocity* began making calls at Elie in 1821, *en route* from Leith to Aberdeen. In June the same year the company announced that the *Tourist* and *Brilliant* steamers calling at Elie would now travel as far north as Inverness. In 1836 a sailing packet carried goods between Elie and Leith twice a week. Leith to Aberdeen steamers called twice and sometimes three times per day, stopping both on their outward and return journeys, and the town was connected to the busy ferry port of Largo by a daily horse omnibus carriage. The Grange Coal Work was established around the same date and by 1854 four pits were operational on the links at Earlsferry, drained by a steam engine near Grangehill. Nine seams of coal were identified, the broadest being eight feet thick, but they were badly faulted and charred in many places by volcanic intrusions, and the workings were finally abandoned around 1860.

Earlsferry once possessed a harbour, formed by the extension of the skerry of rocks which project into the middle of the bay, but the pier was buried by windblown sand in the eighteenth century. The loss of a fishing boat with seven men in 1766 was blamed for the abandonment of the profession in the burgh. The 1837 Statistical Account of Kilconquhar parish mentions that fifteen young men in Earlsferry were employed as weavers. It also states that thirty or forty men formerly went whaling in summer, and that twenty or thirty now went north to the herring fishing in July and August. Although not specifically mentioned it is probable that these were Earlsferry men, as people who lived away from the coast seldom worked at sea.

The boundary between the towns of Elie and Earlsferry was marked by what is now Telfer Wynd. Earlsferry remained part of Kilconquhar parish until 1890, when it was joined with Elie. Both retained separate town councils, however, until the sensible unification of the two into the combined burgh of Elie, Williamsburgh, Liberty and Earlsferry in 1929.

In 1831 the populations of Elie and Earlsferry were 1,029 and 649 respectively, but fifty years later these figures had plunged to just 670 and 286. A lack of local employment played a part. Elie had never embraced the rise of the Forth herring industry with the enthusiasm of its neighbours, and consequently didn't experience the same unprecedented period of growth in the same half century. However, the consolidation of Elie's development as a tourist resort gathered momentum in the 1880s, and by 1901 the combined population of the two towns had risen to 1,142. Growth after this was slow and in 1931 the town contained 1,251 residents. The 1921 census was taken in July and its figure of 2,448 reveals that around 1,000 visitors were in the town in that month. At that time many locals would move into a single room or a shed at the bottom of the garden, and let all or most of their homes to tourists during the summer. This practice, which was discreetly overlooked by the sanitary authorities, continued until well after the war.

Between 1961 and 1971 Elie's population fell from 1,289 to 1,015 as many young people were forced to leave the area to find work and an increasing number of houses became holiday homes. Self-catering holidays caused the hotel trade to dwindle and of the four hotels and fifteen boarding houses in the town in 1951, only two hotels and one guest house now remain. Nonetheless, tourists still play a prominent role in the economy of the town and Elie manages to maintain more shops than most places of comparable size in Fife. In its own very quiet way, Elie is thriving.

A Peep of Elie from Chapel Green

Large quantities of human bones unearthed at both the Earlsferry and North Berwick hospitals have led to the assumption that both institutions had attendant chapels. One of the last sects of the old Celtic church to survive in Scotland was the Culdees, but David I (1124-1153) sought the universal adoption of the church of Rome and confiscated Culdee property. In many cases he downgraded their foundations to hospitals, and it has been suggested that the hospital at Earlsferry, extant by 1154, may have been established by Culdees displaced from their church at Balchristie. I doubt if the Culdees, or the nuns subsequently associated with the hospital, would have approved of the siting of the First World War trophy in the foreground of this 1920s view, although this was removed in the scrap drive during the next conflict.

The 800-ton steamer *Graf Todleben* was carrying 1,800 tons of coal from Methil to her home port of Riga when she ran aground on rocks at Chapel Point at around 3 a.m. on 18 February 1912. The crew launched a distress rocket and sounded her horn, and a crowd of onlookers soon assembled on the shore. The coastguard rocket apparatus was summoned (although in the event this was not actually used), and a line was thrown to the vessel, which lay about 100 yards offshore, by hand. Her eighteen crewmen, however, remained aboard until daybreak and were brought ashore later that day, along with the captain Martin Grieve and his wife. They left for Methil under the care of Mr Romsestrome, the Russian Consul there.

ELIE PIER FROM BEACH

Most of the *Graf Todleben*'s cargo was discharged into lighters the day after the accident. Her bow was high on the rocks and her stern continued to knock against them, and within a week she was a complete wreck. She was eventually freed, and towed to the mouth of Elie harbour where she lay until late September when the wreck was sold to the Port and Clyde Shipping Company. They towed her to Bo'ness for breaking.

Grangehill Farm is on the right of this early 1920s view, and the chimneys of the ruined Grange can be glimpsed behind the cottages on the left. It stands on the site of a building erected for the nuns of North Berwick around the beginning of the thirteenth century. In 1560 the nuns sold Grange to Andrew Wood, vicar of Largo, to pay for repairs to their convent after it was damaged by English raids. Grange was owned by several branches of the Wood family and various other parties before being bought by James Malcolm in 1708. He built the house whose remains survive today. It remained in his family until 1856, and was destroyed by fire in the 1860s.

The 'right of golf' was included in Earlsferry's royal burgh charter of 1589, and the game was certainly being played on the 'Ferry Links' by 1750. The Earlsferry and Elie Golf Club was formed in 1858, and played on an area of ground to the west of Ferry Road. Four members obtained a lease of ground on the east side of the road in 1874, which included the right to build a clubhouse. Two new clubs, Elie Golf House Club and Earlsferry Thistle Golf Club, were formed in 1875; the Ladies' Club was founded in 1884. Membership of the original club dwindled and it was wound up in 1912. This 1904 picture shows the clubhouse in its original form, before considerable additions were made to it in 1906-1907.

Golf Links, (Home Hole) Elie.

Elie's most famous golfer was James Braid, who won the Open Championship on five occasions around the turn of the century. The son of an Elie estate forester, he was born in the house called 'Linmara' on Earlsferry High Street in 1870. He joined Earlsferry Thistle in 1885, and ten years later was closely involved in planning the layout of the new eighteen hole course at Elie. A total of six proprietors owned portions of the course, and in 1973 the Elie Golf House Club purchased each of their shares to ensure its future survival. The presence of builders' hoardings around the site of the Marine Hotel dates this picture accurately to 1904. Sheep, several of which can be glimpsed grazing in the background, were an additional hazard to play at this time!

Sports Club Pavilion, Elie. 45.

Tennis courts were laid out beside the golf course around 1905. The pavilion in this early 1960s view was built in the 1920s, by which time there were eight tennis courts, a bowling green, croquet lawn and even an archery course. Today the pavilion is home to Elie Sports Club, which has a nine hole golf course, 300 yard driving range, putting green, bowling green and five all-weather tennis courts. This quaint little building was relieved of its porch and mock-Tudor timbering during the 1970s.

11

Published by D. M'Dougall, Elie

The recent passage of horses is evident in this turn of the century view of the High Street. One of the children in the background appears to be carrying a spade, and was perhaps sent to retrieve some manure for the roses of 'The Ferry'. The house two doors down from the shop on the left was formerly the Kilconquhar parish manse, which was located in Earlsferry until 1717.

63716.J.V.

Earlsferry post office occupied the building adjacent to the pillar box in this 1909 picture. A sub-office of Elie, it opened on 1 September 1904, closing on 6 June 1975. The associated grocer's shop, the last in Earlsferry, shut a few years later. The forestair on the right was the sole survivor of a campaign of civic improvements carried out by the town council between 1860 and the 1880s, during which time many other such stairs were removed and the street was paved for the first time. These improvements would have been impossible in the 1830s, when the burgh was so decayed that it couldn't even muster enough £10 property owners to form a constituency to elect councillors – a precondition imposed under the terms of several Burgh Reform Acts passed during the reign of William IV.

Earlsferry town hall, on the left of this Edwardian view, was designed by local architect John Currie in 1864 and completed in 1872. It was built on the site of a dilapidated building that dated back to the foundation of the royal burgh. This contained a jail, which the Rev. William Ferrie described as being in a wretched state in 1837, adding that 'fortunately we rarely have occasion to use it'. John Currie (1840-1922) came from a family of Elie builders who built many of the town's nineteenth century houses, including his own residences Gillespie House in South Street (*c.*1870) and Claremont in Bank Street (1897). A cinema was opened in the town hall in 1920 and talking pictures were introduced in 1931.

Guidebooks to Elie proclaimed it to be 'one of the sunniest spots in Scotland', and promised visitors 'it has hardly ever been known to rain here for a whole day'. Just in case all this sunshine tempted holidaymakers away from its churches, visiting evangelical preachers conducted services on the sands to ensure that their spiritual needs were not neglected. This photograph dates from around 1910.

The original Marine Hotel opened in July 1888 and was designed by the architects Burnet & Son & Campbell. On 6 April 1904 a Major Inglis, staying at the hotel, thought he noticed the smell of burning as he retired to his room between 10 and 11 p.m. He thought no more about it, but around 1 a.m. he and his wife awoke with a suffocating feeling and found the building well alight. All 21 visitors and 13 staff in the hotel escaped safely, many only in their nightclothes. Fanned by a strong south-westerly wind, the blaze raged for five hours until only the bare walls remained. This picture of the old Marine Hotel was taken in 1896, and its publication as a postcard in 1914 may well have been an error.

The gutted shell of the Marine Hotel was demolished shortly after the fire and work on a replacement building began in late May 1904. This picture was taken shortly after the new hotel opened for the Easter holidays the following year. In October 1907 the Duchess of Connaught and Princess Patricia spent a week there, and ever after it used the legend 'Patronised by Royalty' in its advertising and stationery.

MARINE HOTEL, ELIE.   B.3525.

The Marine was extended several times and a glass sun veranda added in the 1930s. This 1950 picture shows the building in its completed state as most locals will remember it. From caravan holidays in the 1950s, to the advent of continental package tours, the Marine fell victim to changing holiday fashions and closed in the late 1970s. When permission to demolish it was refused, part of the building was briefly used as a nightclub called Cinderella's. After a disastrous fire in 1983 one wag coined the slogan 'Cinders, the hottest nightspot in town!'. Permission was granted to demolish the hotel in April 1984, and following that the site remained vacant until the houses of Marine Court were erected in 1990.

Elie's first post office was opened in 1797. The present post office, mid-way down the street on the right in this Edwardian view, was built in 1905 and substantially enlarged in 1907. Opposite, the roof of Kirkbrae can be seen peeping through the trees. It was built in the baronial style in 1899 as a private residence for a Professor Greenfield. Mr & Mrs J. B. Greig bought the house in 1920 and converted it into the Golf Hotel, which once boasted a private motor launch for its guests. The hotel was requisitioned during the war, when it was used as a billet for Polish troops. It reopened in 1947 after a major refurbishment and today is the last of Elie's big hotels.

The Wood Memorial Church in Bank Street was named after the Rev. Walter Wood (1812-1882). He was a leading figure in the Disruption of 1843, when a breakaway group from the Church of Scotland formed the Free Church. In the same year he became Elie's first Free Church minister. The original church was designed by a Mr Rochead and was described as a miniature replica of Rosslyn Chapel. It was later used as the Free Church hall, and can be glimpsed on the left of this 1900 view. The new building was designed in 1886 by Sydney, Mitchell & Wilson. In 1949 its congregation was joined, with some resistance, to that of the Parish Church.

A rare interior view of the Wood Memorial Church taken in 1896. The building was demolished in the 1960s, but fortunately its stained glass, including two windows designed by Sir Edward Burne-Jones and executed by Morris & Co. in 1890, was saved and later installed in the Parish Church. Walter Wood has a more enduring memorial in the shape of his book *The East Neuk of Fife*. First published in 1862, a greatly enlarged second edition was published posthumously in 1887. Diligently researched, it is especially strong on local genealogies, and although its depth of information makes it a heavy read it will remain one of the best works of reference ever written on the area.

This photograph, looking west into Earlsferry from the tower of the Wood Memorial Church, predates the building of the Marine Hotel in 1888. It is one of a series of postcards published in 1905 which, although not captioned as such, appear to have been produced as scenes of 'bygone Elie'. Most of the vacant ground between the two towns was developed with villas between 1890 and 1900. The pantiled buildings adjacent to the road on the right housed a brewery and were replaced in 1897 by the villa 'Claremont'.

Bank Street has changed little since this 1904 picture was taken, although the old building next to the shoe shop on the corner was rebuilt the following year. The cobbler's belonged to Robert Don and after his death in 1916 the business was taken over by R. Terras. The building on the left-hand side of the street was formerly the parish school and gave its name to School Street, which was previously known as West Wynd. It is now a hairdresser's, appropriately named Headmasters'.

An 1860s guidebook refers to South Street as an area 'of genteel poverty'. However, this was a positive compliment alongside a popular gazetteer of the 1830s which described Elie as 'exceedingly dull', to the chagrin of the Rev. George Milligan, who defended its honour in the Second Statistical Account. Most of the houses in this 1905 view were built as summer villas on the sites of older properties between 1860 and 1900.

The carved doorpiece belonging to Gillespie House on the extreme left of this 1912 view of South Street is known as the 'Muckle Yett', literally meaning big gate. It was added in 1682 to a building which was already old. This stretched half-way across the street, and was demolished in 1865 to widen the road. The doorpiece bears the initials of Alexander Gillespie and his wife Christian Small. James, Duke of York (later James VII) was governor of Scotland from 1679 to 1682 and lodged in this house on occasions when visiting Sir William Anstruther and the Earl of Balcarres.

THE CASTLE, ELIE, FIFE.   6596. G.W.W.

The oldest part of The Castle in South Street is the tall tower house at its western end, which is thought to date from the sixteenth century. The rest of the building is seventeenth century and may have been erected by its first known owner, Dr John Gourlay, a son of the Kincraig Gourlays, who was recorded as owning the property in 1654. Through the remarriage of his widow the house passed to the Arthurs, a fervent Jacobite family. Two of Patrick Arthur's sons were involved in a plot to capture Edinburgh Castle in 1715. The family were related by marriage to Archbishop Sharp, and it was in this house that his daughter Margaret Sharp learned of her father's murder on Magus Muir near Strathkinness in 1679. The Castle was relieved of the pointy Victorian dormerheads shown in this 1890s photograph during its restoration in 1936.

The old cottages on the left of this 1880s view of Park Place were replaced by a continuation of the adjoining terrace before 1900. Park Place developed along the line of a road from St Andrews to Elie and Largo 'with dykes on either side', which was built in 1774. Other parts of this road were the now private Double Dykes road through Balcarres estate, and the continuation of Colinsburgh's South Wynd to Kilconquhar. 1774 was the year that the Statute Labour system, whereby everyone was legally bound to provide an annual six days' labour on the roads, was replaced by a tax to fund road-building.

The present Elie primary school, on the right of this 1904 picture, was built around 1865 as a replacement for the old parish school in School Street, and a large part of the cost of the building was met by William Baird of Elie House. The parish was relieved of responsibility for the school when the Education Act was passed in 1872; this transferred control of education to school boards under the auspices of local government. The Jacobean style schoolmaster's house to the left of the school was demolished in the 1960s to make way for a new extension.

Elie High Street has changed little since this photograph was taken from the tower of the Wood Memorial Church in the 1880s, but following the building's demolition it is a view no one will ever see again. Rose Cottage, set back from the line of the street on the left, was built around 1840.

Elie Parish Church was completed in 1639. The tower was added at the expense of Sir William Anstruther in 1726, and the building's present appearance dates from a major remodelling in 1831. In 1921 the war memorial was inserted into the corner of the perimeter wall, and has the unusual feature of listing the peacetime occupations of those who fell. One of the names is Lieutenant Rev. W. N. Monteith, the parish minister and Elie's first war victim. He died leading his troops in an assault against German trenches on 25 September 1915.

VICTORIA HOTEL, ELIE.

R.R.R.
E.

The present Victoria Hotel dates from 1840, although there has been an inn on this site for some three centuries. When this photograph was taken around 1910 the hotel was the headquarters of the Scottish Automobile Club and in the 1920s advertised 'horses and carriages of every description for hire'. The building received its mock-Tudor frontage shortly after the last war.

The architectural evolution of Elie High Street is illustrated by this turn of the century postcard; the wall-height of the buildings indicates their age, with the lowest dating from the eighteenth century and the slightly higher ones from the first half of the nineteenth century. The house and shop on the near left were replaced in 1906 by the new premises of Robert Thomson, grocer and wine merchant. Later proprietors of this shop were S. S. Melville in the 1930s and William N. Speed in the 1950s. The old house three doors up from it was completely rebuilt in the early 1950s.

The eighteenth century building on the left of this 1880s view of the High Street and Toll Green was removed in the 1890s to make way for the Queen's Hotel. The present road from Balchristie crossroads to Elie was built as a turnpike road in 1810, and continued along Elie High Street, bypassing St Monans, and joining the 1790-1799 turnpike road from Kirkcaldy via Colinsburgh to Crail, just west of Pittenweem. Two tollhouses were erected on the new road, one at Broomlees and the other at the east end Toll Green. Both seem to have been demolished soon after the abolition of road tolls in Fife in 1878. The cast iron drinking fountain on Toll Green was made at George Smith's Sun Foundry in Glasgow in 1869.

HIGH STREET, ELIE.

Margaret Allan, the sender of this 1911 postcard, stayed at the Wadeslea Dairy which she says was half a dozen yards around the corner from where she has marked a cross at the end of the street. The house on the corner, she adds, belonged to the Elie estate factor. The two men on the right are dressed in the uniform of the North British Railway and the horse and cart across the street from them was the railway lorry, which transported parcels and luggage to and from the station.

Close examination of this aerial view of the Beach Hotel shows that it was still under construction when the picture was taken, dating it accurately to 1931. The middle part of the building with three dormer windows was Elie Lodge, sometimes also styled Elie Cottage, and was built for James Kyd of Woodhill and Cragie in Angus around 1750. It was extended and converted into a hotel by the Beach Hotel Co., who also owned the Marine Hotel. The Beach opened in June 1931, and around 1950 was bought by the Scottish Co-operative Society and renamed Hycroft. They ran it as a convalescent home for their members, but this was closed in the late 1970s. Hycroft was bought by developers and demolition was proposed in 1984. Only the 1931 west wing was retained as part of the subsequent housing development.

Elie station opened on 1 September 1863 when the Leven and East of Fife Railway was extended from Kilconquhar, which had been the terminus since 1857, to Anstruther. The line was taken over by the North British Railway in 1877 and extended to St Andrews six years later. The NBR was swallowed up by the London and North Eastern Railway in 1923, which in turn disappeared with nationalisation in 1948. This picture dates from 1912 and shows the original station building on the left. The building on the opposite platform was added in 1900 and an iron footbridge replaced the wooden one in this view in 1920.

The crossing between Elie and North Berwick is the shortest distance across the Forth east of Burntisland, and in 1845 a proposal was made to build a railway to Elie harbour, where a steam ferry would cross to North Berwick to connect with the main southbound line. Its supporters claimed that it would provide a swift route from north-east Scotland to London and the English markets. However, like many similar proposals in the infancy of Britain's railways, it never made it past the drawing board. The picturesque coastal line from Leven to St Andrews, which included Elie station, was closed to passengers on 6 September 1965.

Elie.

Elie Lodge can be seen in its original condition on the left of this early 1920s view. In the eighteenth century there was a field with a house on it and a road on the seaward side of the Toft gardens. This road ran along the top of a swarf dyke (from the Scots' word 'swarf', meaning to swerve), so-called because of its shape. This was suffering badly from erosion before 1800 and has long since been washed away. Wood expressed the opinion that sand was being blown away from the Elie end of the bay and deposited at Earlsferry and that this was responsible for burying the pier there.

Fisherman's Cottage, Elie

This picture of the Warrender family outside their tiny home at the Toft around 1895 was one of the most popular postcards of Elie in the Edwardian era. The cottage is now used as a store by the Ship Inn. In 1794 Elie had eight fishermen, and they lived rent-free in houses supplied by Sir John Anstruther on condition that they supply the town with fish three times per week. By 1855 there were only six fishermen who manned two small boats under 18 feet keel. A brief attempt to establish a herring fleet saw the number of boats rise to 13 by 1881, but this number had dwindled by the end of the century.

There is no mention of a coastguard at Elie in 1866, but the next available directory lists a James McKinlay of Park Place as coastguard in 1878, and in 1882 William Watty is listed as occupying the coastguard station. The original coastguard houses were the cottages in Admiralty Lane; they were replaced by these buildings at Wadeslea around 1890. A wireless signal station was established between the Ness Lighthouse and the Lady's Tower in 1914 and remained operational until it was closed at the end of World War II. A lookout post was located on the hill behind the wireless station. Elie's last coastguard, Mr J. W. Linton, retired in 1992, and all coastguard operations were subsequently transferred to Leven.

In 1656 Elie was reported to possess two ships of between 40 and 50 tons, but forty years later the harbour was in disrepair. The sandy bay was ideally suited to running ships safely ashore in bad weather, and a petition was laid before the Privy Council in 1696 to repair the harbour. Its members appear to have been swayed by the petitioners, who reminded them that 300 of the king's soldiers would have perished had it not been for the safety and convenience of Elie harbour, and a collection was made for its repair in every parish church in Scotland. This picture was taken in 1896 and shows two Fifie fishing boats in the foreground.

41

The rock on which the granary now stands was formerly an island and could only be reached at low tide. In 1835 a group of gentlemen and farmers of the district invited Robert Stevenson, engineer, to survey the harbour, which had then been in a sorry state for at least forty years. However, his plans were not implemented until William Baird bought the Elie estate in 1853, following which the present causeway and road were completed within two years. This was blamed by many for the silting up of the basin with sand, and by 1900 the harbour was home to just a handful of fishing boats. Potato boats from England, like those in this *c.*1900 view, continued to call in season, but this trade did not resume after the First World War.

Fishing was virtually abandoned in Elie at the start of the First World War, and it never recovered. Old boats were left to rot picturesquely on the foreshore, as illustrated by this early 1920s photograph. By 1928 just six fishermen remained, manning three small boats and landing white fish, crabs and lobsters. When Sir Michael Nairn of Elie House died in 1955, his son Michael George Nairn gifted the harbour to the town council. In 1974 they transferred ownership to the non-profit making Elie Harbour Trust, and in 1993 Baron Vipana, the present holder of the title Baron of Elie & St Monans, gave the trust the outer harbour and anchorage from Elie Ness to Chapel Ness.

Summer excursion steamers began to make regular calls at Elie in the 1870s. From 1877 to 1886 one of the most frequent visitors was George Jamieson's *Fiery Cross*, a small vessel with an absurdly tall funnel, nicknamed the 'floating shebeen'. The only company to develop a fleet of steamers on the Forth was the Galloway Saloon Steam Packet Co., which was formed in 1886. They built a jetty at Apple Rock near the entrance to Elie harbour in 1889, which is shown in this turn of the century picture of their paddle steamer *Wemyss Castle*. Originally called the *Gareloch*, she was built for the North British Railway in 1872. She was renamed when the Galloway S.P. Co. bought the vessel in 1891. The *Wemyss Castle* was broken up in 1906.

STEAMER AT JETTY - ELIE

In 1909 the Galloway S.P. Co. bought the 215 foot *Redgauntlet* from the North British Railway who had owned her since she was built in 1895. She was the steamer most frequently on the Elie sailings until excursions stopped with the outbreak of the First World War. All the Galloway steamers were requisitioned by the admiralty. Many were sunk, and those which were returned after the war were in a sorry state. When the Galloway S.P. Co. was wound up the *Redgauntlet* was sold to an Algerian buyer in 1921. Her registry was closed three years later. Summer cruises to Elie were provided by the Kirkcaldy-owned steamer *Conqueror* from 1922 to 1925, but these marked the end of the excursion trade.

THE JETTY, ELIE,
S.S. ROSLIN CASTLE.

R.R.R.
E.

During the summer months many houses in Elie were let to wealthy Edinburgh businessmen, who would travel back and forward to their offices in the city during the week. In 1887 the Galloway S.P. Co. introduced a daily commuter service from Elie to Leith, but this was reduced to a Monday, Wednesday and Friday service in 1891, and despite protests from passengers was withdrawn altogether at the end of that season. The steel turbine steamer *Roslin Castle* was built for Galloway in 1906 by Hawthorn of Leith. She was sold to the admiralty in 1908 and renamed HMS *Nimble*. Decommissioned in 1922, the steamer changed ownership several times before she was broken up in 1949.

Boys from the *Mars* training ship, photographed at Elie around 1908. The *Mars* was an old naval vessel which was brought to the Tay in 1860 and anchored off Woodhaven near Wormit to serve as a floating reformatory for wayward boys. They were subject to strict naval discipline and were taught a range of practical skills including joinery and seamanship. Every June from 1900 until the *Mars* was scrapped in 1929 the boys spent an annual month's holiday at Elie, where they were accommodated in the old granary at the harbour. Their band provided frequent concerts during their visits and the local papers indicate that the boys were highly thought of by both locals and visitors.

Most of Elie House was built for Sir William Anstruther after he bought the estate in 1697. The projecting wing on the left of this 1915 view was built in 1854-1855 on the site of the original early seventeenth century mansion, which had latterly been used as estate offices. William Baird of Elie House died in 1918 and ten years later his son Captain W. J. Baird sold the Elie estate to Kirkcaldy linoleum magnate Sir Michael Nairn, Bart. The house became the Convent of Marie Reparatrice in the late 1950s and a small chapel was added in 1958. The nuns moved on in the late 1970s and since then the house has lain empty.